FERGUS FALLS M

MW01382893

796.323 CrE
Gumdrop Books
11/2004 $9.21
43213

HORACE GRANT
TRACY McGRADY
NICK ANDERSON
MIKE MILLER
DENNIS SCOTT
ANFERNEE HARDAWAY
RONY SEIKALY
DARRELL ARMSTRONG
GRANT HILL
SCOTT SKILES
SHAQUILLE O'NEAL
BO OUTLAW

THE HISTORY OF THE ORLANDO MAGIC

CREATIVE EDUCATION
JOHN NICHOLS

Published by Creative Education, 123 South Broad Street, Mankato, MN 56001

Creative Education is an imprint of The Creative Company.

Designed by Rita Marshall

Photos by Allsport, Rich Kane, NBA Photos, SportsChrome

Copyright © 2002 Creative Education. International copyright reserved in all countries.

No part of this book may be reproduced in any form

without written permission from the publisher.

Library of Congress Cataloging-in-Publication Data

Nichols, John, 1966- The history of the Orlando Magic / by John Nichols.

p. cm. – (Pro basketball today)   ISBN 1-58341-108-9

1. Orlando Magic (Basketball team)—History—

Juvenile literature. [1. Orlando Magic (Basketball team)—History.

2. Basketball—History.] I. Title. II. Series.

GV885.52.O75 N52 2001   796.323'64'0975924—dc21   00-047327

First Edition 9 8 7 6 5 4 3 2 1

ORLANDO, FLORIDA, LOCATED IN THE CENTER OF THE FLORIDA PENINSULA, WAS NAMED IN HONOR OF ARMY SOLDIER

Orlando Reeves, who was killed during the Seminole Wars of the 1850s. In the last several decades, the community's warm, sunny weather and proximity to some of the world's most beautiful beaches have made Orlando one of the United States' most popular vacation destinations.

Perhaps Orlando's biggest attraction is the famous Walt Disney World amusement complex. Millions of visitors from all over the globe make their way to the theme parks, which include Epcot Center and the Magic Kingdom. Orlando is also home to another kind of Magic—

TERRY CATLEDGE

the Orlando Magic of the National Basketball Association (NBA), who have been thrilling fans for more than a decade.

{THE MAGIC SHOW ARRIVES} Orlando joined the NBA in 1989 as one of two expansion teams. The Magic, along with the Minnesota Timberwolves, built their first roster primarily through an expansion draft in which other teams made aging or unwanted players available. Through the draft, Orlando landed several veterans who would make an impact. Guard Reggie Theus, forward Terry Catledge, and point guard Scott Skiles formed the foundation of the Magic's lineup.

The team also made a solid choice in the 1989 NBA Draft, selecting University of Illinois swingman Nick Anderson. The 6-foot-6 Anderson was known for his versatility. "He can score, he can rebound, and he can play two positions," said Magic head coach Matt Guokas.

The Magic got off to a hot start, scoring more than 100 points in their first 11 games.

NICK ANDERSON

Versatile forward Dennis Scott was a team leader in the Magic's early years.

DENNIS SCOTT

"He'll do a lot of learning this year, but I wish I had his future."

The Magic started their first season well, going 7–7 in their first month. The highlight of the month was the franchise's first win, when Theus scored 24 points to lead Orlando to a 118–110 triumph over the New York Knicks. The rest of the season, however, was a struggle, as the Magic finished with an 18–64 record.

Swingman Otis Smith was one of six players to average at least 13 points a game in **1990–91**.

Orlando added another weapon the next year when it drafted Georgia Tech forward Dennis Scott with its first pick in the NBA Draft. Scott's ability to light up the scoreboard with long-range shooting gave the Magic a much-needed offensive boost. Orlando also received inspired play from the scrappy Skiles, who set an NBA record in 1990–91 by handing out 30 assists in a single game.

Behind these performances, the Magic improved to 31–51.

OTIS SMITH

Scott Skiles's scrappy leadership style made him a fan favorite in the early '90s.

SCOTT SKILES

Although injuries caused Orlando to stumble to a 21–61 mark the next year, the Magic's poor record put them in position to make a move that would change the future of the franchise.

In **1992–93**, the Magic set a franchise record by grabbing 69 rebounds in one game.

{THE SHAQ AND PENNY ATTACK} In 1992, the Magic were awarded the top overall pick in the NBA Draft. With it, the team selected 7-foot-1 and 305-pound Shaquille O'Neal from Louisiana State. The mammoth center was one of the most talked-about players to come along in years. O'Neal's rare combination of immense size and explosive strength had scouts predicting instant stardom.

In his rookie season, O'Neal averaged 23 points, 13 rebounds, and several blocked shots a game and was voted the NBA Rookie of the Year. With his addition, the Magic surged to a much-improved 41–41. "Shaq's a franchise player," said Chicago Bulls head coach Phil Jackson. "Right

SHAQUILLE O'NEAL

now he's just using his size and strength, but as he develops, he's going to become unstoppable."

Going into the 1993 NBA Draft lottery (which determined the

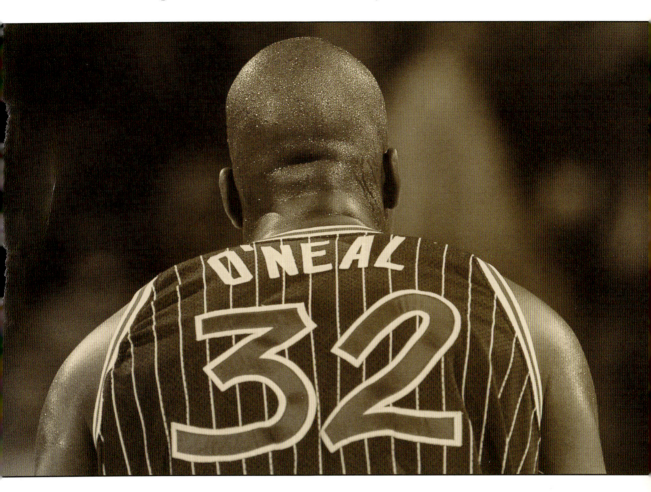

order of top draft picks) the Magic had the best record among non-playoff teams and therefore the smallest chance of winning the first overall pick. Although only 1 of 66 balls in the lottery machine had Orlando's name on it, through a minor miracle, that ball came up first.

The Magic had the first pick in the Draft for the second year in a

For the third straight season, all of the Magic's home games were sold out in **1993–94**.

row, and with it, the team engineered one of the biggest

draft day trades in history. Orlando chose University of

Michigan forward Chris Webber, then traded his rights to

the Golden State Warriors for the rights to Memphis

State guard Anfernee "Penny" Hardaway and three future

first-round picks. The trade delivered Hardaway—the player the Magic

had really wanted—and also ensured that a steady stream of talent

would be rolling into Orlando in the future.

The 6-foot-7 Hardaway was a unique player. Taller than most point

guards, he could easily shoot or pass over his opponent, and he also had

the quickness and ball-handling ability to drive to the basket. With

Hardaway and O'Neal in the same lineup, the Magic suddenly had one

ANFERNEE HARDAWAY

of the league's most potent inside-outside combinations. "I'm glad I'm getting out of this game soon," laughed Los Angeles Lakers forward James Worthy. "I don't want to be around when those two grow up."

In 1993–94, O'Neal and Hardaway led Orlando to a 50–32 record. The young Magic were swept in the playoffs by the more experienced Indiana Pacers, but notice had been served. Orlando was a team on the rise.

{BEAST OF THE EAST} One of the biggest reasons for the Magic's quick postseason knockout in 1994 was the team's lack of a strong power forward. O'Neal was forced to handle much of the rebounding and low-post defense by himself. "Shaq's a great player, but he can't score 30 points a game on offense and still get all the rebounds and block all the shots," said Brian Hill, who had replaced Guokas as head coach. "We needed to get him some help."

Guard Brian Shaw averaged five assists per game off the bench for Orlando in **1994–95**.

That help arrived in the form of forward Horace Grant. The 6-foot-10 Grant had won three NBA championships while playing with Michael Jordan in Chicago, and he brought an intense, winning attitude to his new team. Suddenly, the Magic boasted one of the best starting lineups in the NBA. With Hardaway and Anderson as guards, Scott and Grant as forwards, and O'Neal manning the pivot, the Magic had the

BRIAN SHAW

Shaquille O'Neal turned the Magic into an Eastern Conference powerhouse.

look of an All-Star team. In 1994–95, Orlando shot out to a 23–6 start and never faltered on its way to a conference-best 57–25 mark.

Blue-collar forward Horace Grant added muscle to Orlando's low post for five seasons.

In the playoffs, the Magic powered their way to the NBA Finals, where they faced Hakeem Olajuwon and the defending champion Houston Rockets. In game one at the Orlando Arena, O'Neal and Hardaway each scored 26 points, but the Rockets pulled out a 120–118 overtime victory. The narrow defeat seemed to deflate the young Magic, who lost the next three games and the series. After the series, an emotional O'Neal voiced his frustration with the team's poor performance. "It's a hard loss to take," he said. "I thought this was our year."

The next season, the Magic returned stronger than ever, determined to prove that their march to the 1995 Finals was no fluke. Although O'Neal missed the first 22 games with a thumb injury, his

HORACE GRANT

teammates carried Orlando to a 17–5 start in his absence. The Magic were driven largely by the deadly long-range gunning of Scott, who set an NBA record by pouring in 267 three-pointers during the season.

Orlando finished the season with a 60–22 mark—second only to the Chicago Bulls' 72–10 record.

All season long, fans had expected that the Magic and Bulls would meet in the Eastern Conference Finals, and the two powerhouses didn't

disappoint. Orlando lost game one 121–83, but it also lost Grant to an

Reserve center Jon Koncak helped Orlando go 37–4 on its home court in **1995–96**.

elbow injury. Without his inside contributions, the Magic

were no match for the eventual NBA champion Bulls,

who swept Orlando in four games.

{PENNY IN COMMAND} The playoff loss to the

Bulls was painful, but the Magic franchise was dealt a

much more devastating blow when O'Neal left town in the off-season

to join the Los Angeles Lakers as a free agent. Left without a force in

the middle, the Magic turned to Hardaway for leadership. The guard

had established himself as an All-Star, and it was clear that the team's

fate rested on his shoulders. "It's Penny's team now, and we'll go as far as

he takes us," Grant said.

To ease Hardaway's load, Orlando acquired veteran center Rony

JON KONCAK

Rony Seikaly replaced O'Neal in **1996–97**, averaging 17 points and 9 boards a game.

RONY SEIKALY

Seikaly to help fill the hole left by O'Neal's departure. After a knee

injury sidelined Hardaway, however, the team stumbled. With Orlando's

record at 24–25, Coach Hill was fired and replaced by

assistant Richie Adubato. The team responded well to the

change, bouncing back to go 21–12 the rest of the way.

In the 1997 playoffs, the Magic faced the favored

Miami Heat in the first round. The Magic had a healthy

With his great leaping ability, Bo Outlaw was a top-notch shot blocker and dunker.

Hardaway back in the lineup, but the Heat took the first two games

with ease. With his team facing elimination, Hardaway poured in 42 and

41 points to lead Orlando to victory in the next two games. In game

five, however, the Heat held on for a 91–83 victory.

{REBUILDING WITH DALY} Before the 1997–98 season, the

Magic hired Chuck Daly as their new head coach. Daly had led the

Detroit Pistons to two NBA titles in the late 1980s, and Orlando fans

BO OUTLAW

counted on him to rebuild the struggling Magic. Unfortunately, injuries then hit the team, sidelining both Hardaway and Anderson.

Without their stars, the Magic battled furiously to remain in the

playoff race. Under Daly's steady guidance, players such as forwards Derek Strong and Charles "Bo" Outlaw and guard Darrell Armstrong led the Magic to a respectable 41–41 mark. "I'm very proud of these guys," said Coach Daly. "They could have quit when Nick and Penny were hurt, but they gave me all they had."

Daly's second season at the helm was shortened to 50 games due to unrest between NBA players and owners that resulted in a lockout. When the season finally got underway, the Magic bolted to a 33–17 record. In the playoffs, they faced the Philadelphia 76ers and star guard Allen Iverson. After the teams split the first two games, Iverson led the 76ers to a convincing series victory. "It's a big disappointment," Anderson said. "I thought we were a better team than this."

After the season, Daly decided to retire from coaching. The Magic were left with an even bigger hole to fill when Hardaway told the team he wanted to be traded. The relationship between the player and the team's management had soured during his injury-plagued seasons.

Michael Doleac and John Amaechi were part of a rebuilt Magic front-court in the late **'90s**.

MICHAEL DOLEAC

Orlando then dealt Hardaway to the Phoenix Suns for forwards Pat

Garrity and Danny Manning and two future first-round draft picks.

Journeyman forward Chris Gatling led all Orlando players in rebounds per game in **1999–00**.

{ROLLING WITH RIVERS} In 1999, the Magic made a bold move, hiring former NBA guard and television analyst Glenn "Doc" Rivers as the team's new head coach. Rivers had no previous coaching experience, but during his 13-year playing career he had earned respect as a team leader and a student of the game.

The 38-year-old Rivers had played in the league until 1996 and

figured to be a more effective communicator than the more old-

fashioned Daly. Rivers's low-key style and patience proved to be the

perfect tonic for the young Magic. Predicted by many experts to finish

near the bottom of their division, the Magic overachieved on almost

every level during the 1999–00 season.

CHRIS GATLING

Without a marquee player to revolve around, Orlando shared the ball and pressured opposing teams with ferocious defense. Armstrong, Outlaw, and center John Amaechi emerged as the leaders on a team that fought hard every night on its way to a 41–41 record. After the team's surprisingly strong season, Rivers was named NBA Coach of the Year.

In 2000, the Magic rebuilt in a major way through the free agent market, signing superstar forward Grant Hill and explosive swingman Tracy McGrady. In the 2000 NBA Draft, the Magic continued to load for the future by picking up talented young forward Mike Miller. "Last year we built a nucleus of guys that work hard every night and do the little things," explained Coach Rivers. "Now with the addition of Hill and McGrady, we have the weapons necessary to win the big games."

Darrell Armstrong was again among the NBA's steals leaders in the **2000–01** season.

DARRELL ARMSTRONG

Like Anfernee Hardaway, Tracy McGrady was an explosive scorer and playmaker.

TRACY McGRADY

The Magic counted on All-Star forward Grant Hill to lead them into the 21st century.

GRANT HILL

For more than a decade, the Magic have been the model for building a successful team from the ground up. Through good times and bad, Orlando's fans have never wavered in their support of the young franchise. With Orlando's roster of talented players, opponents may need a bit of magic themselves to stop the Magic in the seasons ahead.

FERGUS FALLS MIDDLE SCHOOL

The history of the Orlando Mag

796.323 Cre   43213

Nichols, John.
Fergus Falls Middle School